Copyright © 2020 Olivi

How to Market your Music on a Budget by Olivia Dunn © 2020 Olivia Dunn

All rights reserved.

No portion of this book may be reproduced in any form without permission from the publisher, except as permitted by UK copyright law.

All links were correct at the time of going to print, and I am not affiliated with any of them.

For permissions contact olivia@oliviadunn.co.uk

www.oliviadunn.co.uk

Acknowledgements

Thank you to the bands, promoters, agents, managers and others in the marketing/music industry who have given me a load of inside info and offered their words of wisdom, in particular Vicky Whitlock at Firebrand Music, Steve Knightley of Show of Hands and Matt Bartlett of Midnight Mango.

Thanks also go to my brilliantly creative family who are always there for a sense-check or a dose of encouragement.

This is for Lily Juno.

CONTENTS

Copyright	1
Dedication	3
Chapter One: Introduction	7
Chapter Two: The basics	11
Chapter Three: Your band biography	25
Chapter Four: Social media	29
Chapter Five: Website	37
Chapter Six: Photos and videos	44
Chapter Seven: Media (digital, print and radio)	47
Chapter Eight: Networking	51
Chapter Nine: Mailing Lists and Newsletters	54
Chapter Ten: Getting Gigs	58
Chapter Eleven: Post-Covid and Beyond	67
Resources	69
About The Author	71

CHAPTER ONE: INTRODUCTION

Playing music that you love with people that you (hopefully!) love too is incredibly satisfying and it can lead to many memorable adventures – good and bad. Adventures that will live with you your whole life, and that you will enjoy reliving time and time again. I've never met a soul who regretted being in a band, even if it was sometimes at the expense of getting a 'real job'.

It's certainly never time wasted; at worst it is character-building, and when things are going right it's ridiculously exciting and incredibly satisfying.

As anyone in a band will tell you, for every magical, life-affirming moment on-stage there is a whole lot of work that goes on behind the scenes. It's work that you do gladly (for the most part) if you're passionate about getting your music heard. But marketing and promoting a band takes a lot of time and it is easy to spend time getting lost down the wrong rabbit holes.

This backstage work can be time-consuming, and it tends to generally fall to the one or two members of the band who are truly committed and who have the necessary skills to keep the wheels turning.

This book is written for the grafters; those hard-workers, the passionate musicians who are so dedicated that they spend all their spare time (and for the most part unpaid) rehearsing, writing and getting gigs. It's written to help you maximise the time you spend marketing and promoting your band in the right ways to the right people, so that you can free up more time for the fun bits.

I can't tell you how many bands I have encountered over the years who are exceptional at what they do, but you wouldn't know it if you searched for them online.

I'm talking bands who could easily be world-famous if they only **sorted our their online profile**. Bands that you can't find on social media, biographies that are unfinished and packed full of hackneyed clichés, websites that are years out of date, grainy promo shots and dodgy videos taken with smartphones dominating YouTube.

It breaks my heart that these talented people tend not to get anywhere simply because they don't understand **how to market themselves**.

I also spent a few years running a music booking agency, and all my suspicions were confirmed during this time. I couldn't offer work to a band who had a terrible/non-existent online profile, no matter how good I *knew* they were, because I knew full well that they would be impossible to sell to a client who hadn't seen them live.

It's all very well me saying, 'They're brilliant', but people want the proof, and I suppose if I were the client I would feel exactly the same.

Without the right marketing materials, a full press kit and a professional image there was simply nothing I could do for these bands. I yearned for bands who were as good online as they were live, but there was always a massive shortage. The agency didn't last long!

Of course, there are the bands who break the mould. The ones who appear from nowhere with no marketing, no website, secret gigs and an intentional social media black-out where nobody can find out anything about them. This in itself is a very clever marketing trick, but it's rare and I suspect the budget behind the scenes to make something like this work is massive.

This book is designed to give you the tools and knowledge to promote yourself in the usual way – and on a limited budget. It's a great idea to pay attention to how other bands are marketing themselves – you'll pick up loads of ideas along the way.

My message is a clear and simple one – if you want to sell your band to people then **make your product easy to sell.**

So what sort of skills are needed to market and promote your music? Well, there are a lot. You need to be a fantastic writer, a great designer, a website builder, a social media expert, you need to understand your market and you need to be a fantastic networker.

If you are not these things yourself then you need the money to outsource it (and we can add photographers and videographers to that list too).

This all sounds daunting I know, and many bands place all of this stuff into the hands of someone else (often at great expense). But the good news is that there are shortcuts and workarounds to be found here, there and everywhere. In this book I will show you how you can be your own marketing agency for a fraction of the cost, and in doing so remain in control of your own destiny.

By trade I'm a writer, but I have spent my life playing fiddle in bands at every level, so I understand the industry in which you're working. I've spent a lot of time chasing gigs, marketing and promoting, sleeping on sofas and travelling in the back of Transit vans.

My day job these days is as Head of Marketing for a management consultancy, so I also understand where you need to be and how you need to get there.

As a side hustle, I use my knowledge and skills to write resonant press kits, biographies, social media content and tour/album press releases for bands at the top of their game. I've seen the very best of marketing and the very worst of marketing along the way

– and learned a lot from both.

A word of warning…

Being a talented musician is just the start of running a band. There are a whole host of other skills that you need to develop and refine if you want to take your music further. As a word of warning, if you don't develop these marketing and promotion skills yourself then you'll find there are plenty of people along the way who want to jump on your 'band-wagon' and help you out.

This is great if they can put their money where their mouth is, but if they aren't as good as they say they are (and believe me, people can really 'talk the talk' when they need to) then they are just another mouth to feed, and we all know there doesn't tend to be a lot of cash spare.

The more you can do yourself, the better. This is not just to save time, but also to keep control of the direction of your band. There is no doubt that a manager, an agent and a promoter can give you a huge leg-up, but you are far more likely to attract the good ones if you present them with a product that comes with its own growing audience.

They will be impressed and reassured by you if they see that you're already all over your marketing, and from their point of view it's less work for them to do if you've got your promotion sorted already.

I really hope that by following the tips in this book you can take your band to the next level and get your music heard by as many ears as possible!

CHAPTER TWO: THE BASICS

What's in a name?

One of the most crucial elements of your marketing is **your band's name**. Down the line, it can be very hard to change if you've got it wrong, so if you are in the early stages of setting up a band then it's a missed opportunity not to give this serious thought and get it right.

The right name should be:

- Original
- Memorable
- Easy to spell (for online searches)
- Easy to pronounce
- Not used anywhere else
- Short and snappy
- Evocative of what you do – consider the mood of your music

Of course, there are plenty of band names that don't fit these criteria, but it's a good place to start.

People use all sorts of different inspirations for their band name. It could be a character from a book you love, something from nature that inspires you, or anything else that matters and has meaning to you in some way. The important thing is that it's original.

When thinking up your band name, it's a good idea to check if a relevant website URL (website address) is available. Also, check that it is not trademarked by someone else already, so you can be sure it is legally available.

I mentioned above that your band name should be short and snappy – this is not just so that it is memorable, but also because a long band name is a nightmare to try and fit on merchandise like badges.

Before you finalise your band name, scour Google, YouTube, Facebook etc just in case someone's already using the name. It's a pain if you discover it's already been taken, but it will save you a lot of hassle in the future.

Try it out on a few friends too to see what they think. A sense-check at this point is a very good idea – before you find out your shiny new band name means something really offensive in another language for example!

Buy the relevant domain name as soon as possible, even if you don't have a website yet – all of that will come in time but it will stop it from being snapped up by someone else in the meantime. You should expect to pay no more than around £10 per month for your domain name (and often it's even less).

If the one you want is more expensive than that then it's better to find out earlier rather than later so you can think of a different name.

There's more on websites later on in this book.

A quick word about using your own name as your band name. It is done frequently, but if you change your name (e.g. you get married and choose to lose your maiden name) you will cause yourself hassle.

It should go without saying that if the band name is your name, then you'll be expected at every gig. So if you're ill or otherwise unavailable then the gig will likely need to be pulled, whereas otherwise it might be possible to get a dep (deputy) musician in to fill your place.

The big bits

Your top-line messaging starts with your band name and from there it's all the other important information that you need to get across. It's easy to forget this important stuff when you're in the weeds of social media, so write a list of all the crucial information that people need/want to know, along the following lines:

- Line up details (including names, instruments, brief bios)
- Where you're based
- What genre you fall into
- What sort of venues you tend to play
- Biggest gig/achievement to date, awards, etc.
- Quotes from reviews etc.

Have all this information in a central place so you always have the most recent version of it to hand for when you are doing any marketing. This is called your '**boilerplate content**'; the words you can use over and over again, for example as the basis of a press release.

Nailing all of this down early brings the following advantages:

a)   You're not constantly writing and rewriting the same things.
b)   You keep a level of consistency across all platforms.

As and when you need to update your boilerplate content, do it all in one place and keep a list of all the places that need updating so that old content isn't still hanging around on your Facebook bio for example.

The brand

Your band is a brand, and it's a great idea to start seeing it that way. It needs a visual identity to stick in people's minds. Outside of music think of Coca-Cola, Nike, Vodafone... three very memorable brands that stand out visually because they have spent a LOT of money honing their identity. The colours, the fonts and the straplines have all been given a great deal of thought.

Within the music industry think of the Beatles, Oasis, Pink Floyd. All of them have logos that stick in your mind. They aren't fancy, they just have a certain 'something'.

Every band needs a logo. That's the emblem (or just your band name in a distinctive font) that people will be greeted with on your posters, your website, your social media... everywhere. Make it good. It doesn't have to cost a lot – if you aren't naturally gifted in the design department yourself then you can work with freelance designers on sites like Fiverr and often that will turn up a great idea or two. If you have any marketing budget at all, this is the area to spend it on.

The most effective logos are the simplest. Nike's 'tick', Vodafone's 'comma' and the Beatles' name in an easily recognisable font are all great examples of this.

Once your logo is established give some thought to other basic **branding guidelines**. Give yourself a 'house style' - a colour palette of three or four colours to work with (make sure you write down the colour references so you use the same shade each time). Pick a font that you will use for website copy and tour posters, and stick to it. Too many fonts in one place can be confusing to look at.

While we are talking fonts, it's worth saying that the font that you pick should be a simple one. If it's too fancy or swirly, you'll risk making posters etc. hard to read.

Giving yourself some branding/design parameters for posters and other collateral will help you maintain a consistent brand. Consistency is reassuring and recognisable.

It also means that you do not have to start from scratch every time you are designing a poster or something – you already know roughly what goes where. Have a look at other gig posters and ask yourself what works, and what doesn't.

Once you have decided how you want to come across, write it down. This is a central place where you make a note of your fonts, colour palette and logo, so that you have it all in one place when you need it. You can also send this to anyone who ends up doing any work for you.

When it comes to branding, consistency is everything. Spending some time getting your branding right is a great investment. You can always change it in the future, but if your central branding guidelines and checklist are in place then it will make any updates far easier.

The 4 Ps of marketing

I'm a creative and therefore not a fan of 'one-size-fits-all' theories, frameworks and methodologies. But a basic understanding of marketing principles is useful, so stick with me.

There is some truth in some basic marketing principles which can be applied to pretty much anything. I'm not going to go into too much detail, and you can search online for more resources, but I do think it's helpful to give an overview of the 4Ps: **Price**, **Place**, **Product** and **Promotion**.

If you spend time considering and optimising your 4 Ps it will stand you in good stead as you push your music out into the world.

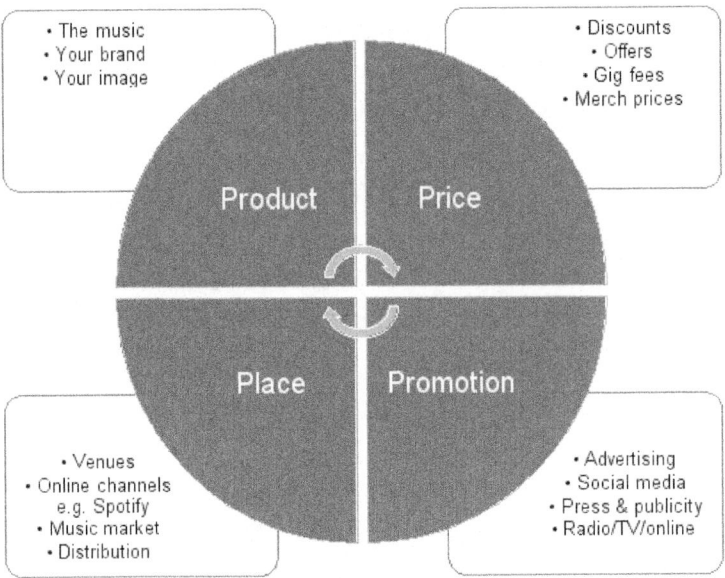

Fig 1: The 4 Ps of Marketing

Product

Your product is first and foremost your music. Be really clear in your mind about what that is, so you understand where best to position it. Don't release anything you're not proud of – a rough demo can still be kicking around online and haunting you years later!

What makes your particular product unique? In marketing people talk about a 'USP' – **Unique Selling Point**. What it is that your music does that nobody else's does? Understanding this is a very important part of your marketing strategy, and it will help you summarise what makes you special when put on the spot.

Consider your **image** too. Of course, many bands are known for their image even more so than their music, and this won't be a new concept to you. But it's worth giving it some thought. Perhaps there's a dress code on stage? Maybe you'll brand the kick drum with your band logo? How do you come across to your audience?

Tangibly, your product might be a CD or vinyl, and less tangibly it might be a download or simply a wonderful live music experience. Consider what it is you are offering the world, where it fits and how you can improve on it to add value.

Your product should be really **easy to access**. Whether it's a gig ticket, a physical CD sale or an online download make sure the sales process is flawless and efficient, otherwise you'll see people abandoning their baskets.

Test any new product on a small, trusted audience before throwing a lot of money and time at promoting it. For example, if you design a new t-shirt then get a couple printed and show them to friends etc before placing a huge bulk order.

Have a look at similar bands to you and watch how they are marketing their product. Ask yourself what you like about it, and what you don't like. Are they getting an impressive engagement online? Do loads of people turn up at their gigs? You can learn a lot from those doing similar things around you.

And then have a look at the big bands – the ones who have really 'made it', selling out stadiums and performing internationally. They will have had big bucks spent on every element of their product. How have they positioned their music, their image and their brand? Why do so many people buy t-shirts with their logo on it?

And finally, always keep this question in mind: '**How can I make my product better?**'. Perhaps you could improve the recording quality of a CD, or include a limited edition insert, or sign the CDs before you sell them? No matter what aspect of your product you are considering, there are always ways in which to add value and improvement.

This is the creative process in a nutshell – always strive to be better.

Price

Often your price is the last thing you consider when thinking about your marketing. But giving it some thought now will pay dividends in the long run.

A lot of bands start out playing for free, and this is great for gaining exposure and building your audience. Playing for free is a great way of building experience if you are not quite at the level where you believe you are delivering value by charging. I've done plenty of free gigs, and I still do – but these days I am more selective about where and how I donate my time and skills.

When setting your gig fees it's important to be realistic, but also to **know your value**.

Put yourself in the shoes of whoever is booking you for a moment. What do they stand to get out of you playing at their event/festival/party? Do you fall under the 'entertainment category' (mainly covers, upbeat, dancing music)? If so, you are providing a service, so charge accordingly.

If you're in it to push your original material then your price should reflect this. It's sad but true that, especially when starting out, cover bands can expect to earn a lot more than original bands. And original bands will probably find themselves at a lot of open mic nights, playing for free and building their following before being able to move up the ranks. There are of course always exceptions to this.

I will mention charity gigs because it comes up a lot. If you are approached to do a gig for free to benefit the charity then bear in mind that every other service they use will be paid for (think toilet hire, bar staff, venue hire, catering). There simply isn't the expectation that these service providers will do this for free, but unfortunately that expectation *is* there for bands.

It's totally your call, but a good charity event's ticket prices should cover its costs, so never feel guilt-tripped into playing for free when a polite 'no' would do the job. You will likely hear the word 'exposure' come up in these conversations a lot, and only you can decide if the exposure you get in return is worth the time, effort and energy of providing a service for free.

Do give pricing lots of thought, know your value and if someone is making money from you then make sure you're making money too. Only agree to play free gigs if there is **a lot in it for you**.

Having a clear idea of your pricing structure will help you position yourself against similar bands. For example, if you charge £500 for a standard gig then have a look at the other bands who charge around the same, and make it your mission for your marketing to be better than theirs!

I don't like the term 'competitor', but like it or not the other bands who share your space in the market are your competitors. That said, it's well worth getting to know them and keeping an eye on their marketing activity and fee structure.

While they may be competing for work in the same space as you, don't see them as rivals - it may be that you can pass gig opportunities back and forth to one another. The music world is also a small world, and there's every chance you might end up on the same bill or even playing in the same band as them in the future.

While a general fixed fee is a good thing to have in mind, be prepared to be **flexible** on that. For example, Glastonbury Festival is notoriously hard to get a gig at, and unless you're very lucky you can forget being paid for it while at grassroots level. But I don't know many bands who wouldn't jump at the chance of playing such an iconic festival, regardless if they're being paid for it or not.

Then, of course, there is the price of your music, your gig tickets (if you have a say in that) and your downloads and merch to consider. It's easy to underprice or overprice, but if you're not getting the sales you'd like then don't blame it all on price. Your marketing strategy might not be working well enough for you.

Your sales (tickets, merch, CDs, downloads combined) will start to tell you a lot about what is and isn't working in your marketing strategy. Keep a keen eye on the numbers **and look for patterns**.

Special offers and discounts can be a great way of boosting sales – especially seasonally e.g. in the run-up to Christmas. Offering a half-price t-shirt with every CD sale is a great way of upselling. The more creative you are with your price promotions the better, but make sure any deal is easy to understand and well-publicised.

Place

Of course, the most important location that you will gain exposure is at **a live gig**. This could be at a live music venue, but it could also be at a wedding, a party, a pub, a festival or even on the street while busking. There is nothing better for building a fan base than playing in people's home town.

Don't expect your target audience to go out of their way to come to you – you need to go to them. **A tour** is a great way of getting the word out and building followers, and if you're not quite ready for a tour of music venues then a busking tour is a great idea, and a whole lot of fun too.

But there are other very important locations away from where you play your live music to consider.

Give the **social media channels** that you use some thought. There was a time when SnapChat was going to be *the* future of marketing, and that hasn't really happened. Not so far anyway. Maintaining a million social media channels is time-consuming and boring, so pick one or two that work best for you. I'll talk more about this later on, but I still think that Facebook, Instagram and perhaps to a lesser extent Twitter are the places bands should focus on.

Your 'place' is also **your gigs**, so if you're a 'sit down and listen' kind of band then don't pitch for weddings, pub gigs and other noisy events. It's not fair on them and nobody will come away with what they wanted. Think carefully about the venues you want to play in, and where your music is most likely to go down well.

Online channels such as Spotify, YouTube and iTunes are also your 'place', and while it takes some time to figure out how to get your music on there it's essential to make your product easily accessible in all formats. You'll likely never make your millions from Spotify, and there are good arguments for and against using it, but it's certainly worth considering.

And finally – your 'place' is also **your stage**, so give plenty of thought to your set-up and how you come across to the audience. The simple addition of a drum riser and a branded kick drum can make you look a whole lot more professional.

Promotion

This includes all the tools you use to promote your music – and is predominantly what this book will focus on so I won't go into too many more details here. The main message to take away here is that you **must promote yourself**.

Once you've considered and optimised your place, your price and your product, it's time to consider how you're going to promote it. Social media is the obvious place to start when it comes to plugging a gig, but beyond this you can pay a local promoter to help (often a venue will have their own promoter who can help).

Think about your **target audience** and consider where they hang out – both online and in real life. Those places should be the places you focus on when it comes to promoting your music. What social media channels do they typically use? What time of day might they most regularly use them?

The world is split into people who love shouting about who they are and how good their music is, and those who cower any time the opportunity to shout about themselves occurs. In my experience the best music often comes from those who let it speak for itself, but in this day and age, you need to be a bit bolder and learn how to promote yourself, or more specifically, your music.

It may help you to know that it takes the same message to be repeated **approximately seven times** before it is heard, remembered and retained. So right at that point that you feel like you're being a repetitive bore is when your message is starting to get through.

Getting a press release into a newspaper (online or digital) is great promotion, as is performing live on a radio station or other online channel. Think of as many ways and as many places as possible to promote yourself.

Try and secure yourself a few interviews, whether it's in-person at a gig or festival, or in print on a website.

And what is the most effective promotion method of all? **Word of mouth.** Ask your fans to spread the word about your music, as they are the best ambassadors of your brand that you could wish for.

What's Your Story?

So that's some marketing theory for you. I would also add one more thing to think about.

The best marketing is really just storytelling. What is it about your music that makes you stand out? Perhaps you have a funny gig anecdote that you could use? Or maybe you are using a new approach that nobody has tried before?

The best example of this is Sandy Thom, who streamed live gigs from her bedroom, or garage or whatever. She wasn't the first person to do this, but it became her story because all her marketing messages reinforced this. She became forever known as the first artist to build her own internet audience organically. Whether this is true or not isn't really the point – she got the story right.

I worked with a band who had once (before my time with them) parked their tour bus on a beach, had a bit of a party and neglected to notice the tide coming in. Once Mother Nature had done her thing, all that remained was approximately half a metre of the bus's roof – the rest was submerged. Obviously this was a bit of a disaster for the band, and a very expensive mistake. Loads of precious instruments were destroyed, and the van was a write-off. But the promotion at the time was off the scale, and 15-odd years later it's an anecdote that people still talk about, and that still features in their marketing: https://www.maddogmcrea.co.uk/about. Gold dust.

Spend some time thinking about what makes you different. Is there a disaster that you can turn into a triumph?

If you build it, they will come

Building a brand is a crucial element of any business. Spend time building your audience not just in real life, but also online, and provide a 'home' for them on Facebook so they feel part of your community. The larger your audience, the more people you can sell to (not just tickets to events, but also downloads, CDs and other merchandise).

Think of it as less of an audience, more of a community. By making your fans feel engaged and valued you are really making a huge difference. If it feels like a genuine and authentic, two-way relationship, it will serve you well and provide a solid foundation on which to build.

One more thing…

The Musicians' Union is an organisation set up to support anyone working in the industry. For a modest annual subscription you'll get access to a wealth of resources and support when you need it the most. They are very helpful for times when fees go unpaid, bookings get cancelled or when you want to find out more about protecting your intellectual property.

You'll also get access to instrument and Public Liability insurance, free advice, legal assistance, workshops, networking events and industry news. I'm not connected with them in any way, but I would recommend having a look at the benefits of joining and deciding if it's right for you.

CHAPTER THREE: YOUR BAND BIOGRAPHY

Your band bio is one of the most crucial elements of your press kit. It will be used EVERYWHERE – both online and in real life, so it's really important to get it right. It must convey what you want it to, tell readers what they want and need to know, and not make you cringe every time you see it pop up!

Venues tend to use the first 80-100 words of your bio and this is one of the very many reasons it is worth keeping it short and snappy. Anything past 100 words isn't likely to be read anyway. You can expand on it for your website's 'About Us' page, and this can be used for lengthier interviews and editorial. But those 100 words will form the basis for everything.

Write three bios, each that build upon each other:

- Bio 1:   50 words (for venues etc.)
- Bio 2:   100 words (for social media etc.)
- Bio 3:   5-6 paragraphs (for press releases and the bio page on your website.

Your full biography should include these elements:

1. Band name (sounds obvious, but never miss a chance to get the name mentioned)
2. An attention-grabbing introduction
3. Your background as a band
4. What makes you stand out/different
5. Description of your music and genre
6. Any awards, career highlights/achievements
7. Media quotes (or a testimonial from someone well-known)
8. The most up to date info (latest gigs, album etc).

When considering what makes a great band biography, it is useful to know what doesn't work.

Firstly, have a blanket cliché ban. For example, the phrase 'self-penned' should be banned – it's totally overused, lazy and boring, and just one example of many, many clichés that creep into band biographies.

Find more inventive ways to say the same thing (but avoid flowery language too).

Secondly, nobody really cares about things like how long your band has been going or what your influences are. Don't compare yourself to anyone else or claim to be the 'next' anybody. You are you, and there is nobody like you.

Phrases like, 'Fans of Bob Dylan will love this band', is, in my opinion, a little bit lazy too, but I do understand why people use it – it does at least start to summarise the music.

To a promoter, an agent, a live music venue or any other music industry professional, coming across a **fully original and engaging band biography** is a rare joy.

Don't mention how hard it is to pigeonhole your music into one particular genre either, as pretty much every band has this issue. It is useful to at least nod to the genre that most accurately describes your style – just don't get hung up on it.

Try and write it in your own **'tone of voice'** as it will sound more authentically 'you'. I can spot a bio that an agent or promotor has written a mile off. There is room here for a subtle display of creativity so try to strike that balance of imparting the information you need to get across while putting your own individual stamp on it.

Top tip >> *To boost your biography's individuality there is a very easy trick that I use quite a lot. By nature, we all tend to write things in certain orders by default. So, say for example your bio is three sentences over 100 words. Try taking the last sentence and putting it first. A simple tweak like this can transform a boring bio to something unique.*

Don't try and cram too much information in; this is not the place to go into detail. Pick three things you want people to know about your music and stick to them.

In business networking it's called an **'elevator pitch'** – imagine you are in an elevator with someone and they ask, 'So what do you do?' You have two minutes to tell them. This sounds really easy, but you'd be amazed how many people waffle either in writing or in speech at this point. To be able to adequately sum up/sell your brand in a couple of minutes is harder than it sounds and doing some work on it will help you a lot.

Once you have hit on the bios that work for you, keep them to hand and copy and paste them everywhere – your social media, your website, your CDs – everywhere. The more people see the same message being repeated, the more it will resonate. Don't end up with five different versions of the same biography.

Marketing is all about reinforcing a **consistent message**, so just keep on keeping on. Your bio won't work for you forever and it'll need refreshing from time-to-time, so make sure it is updated once every six months or so with any latest tour/album news, and any new career highlights etc.

CHAPTER FOUR: SOCIAL MEDIA

Love it or hate it, there's no denying that social media is fantastic for building an audience and spreading the word about what it is that you do. The potential for reach is massive, and it doesn't have to take ages to get right either.

In this section I'm going to assume you have at least a basic level of knowledge about social media, as the majority of people do. If you are starting from scratch, then I suggest you do a couple of online training courses to get up to speed on the basics – there are plenty of free ones online.

In general, different platforms work for different industries and audiences. For example, I find LinkedIn extremely useful for the 'day job' but I wouldn't even consider plugging gigs there – there just isn't the interest for it, and it's not why it was designed. I do see lots of freelance musicians, engineers, producers, lighting engineers and the like on LinkedIn, but never, ever bands.

For music, I believe **Facebook** is your most powerful tool.

You can link this in with Instagram very easily so you're only ever updating one platform. However, linking your social media platforms is not always a great idea. Each platform is different, with ones like Facebook not really being onboard with hashtags, and others like Instagram focusing on images, not copy.

For this reason, I prefer not to link accounts. It's a bit more work, but the social media output is more effective for it. I use Buffer to schedule and tweak posts across all the platforms I use instead.

If you use social media management software like **Buffer** or **Hootsuite** (and plenty of other similar platforms that are available too) you can update all of your social media accounts in one place. This can save a lot of time and hassle.

In this book I focus on Facebook, but I also recommend you consider using Twitter and Instagram too.

There are plenty of resources online about how to set up a band Facebook page. It's worth doing your research first so you set up a **public Facebook page – not a Facebook group**.

I have seen bands set up groups on Facebook where you have to request to join to see the content. Anything that requires any extra effort from casual browsers is likely to put them off, and a page is the best way to hook them in. All they should need to do is click 'like'.

A few quick and dirty Facebook tips for musicians:

- Sort the URL - this is the web address of your Facebook page. It should be the same as your band name, and you'll find how to do this in the settings.

- Use the band logo as the 'thumbnail' image, and upload a good quality cover banner too – perhaps a picture of the band or the cover of your latest album.

- Make use of relevant hashtags on all of your social media accounts – they can be very helpful indeed, especially on Instagram. If you have an album or tour coming up then give it a hashtag so that you can track mentions of it online.

- You can set up an 'event' via your Facebook page for every gig, which people can like and share, and it'll send them reminders too.

- You can also line up a run of scheduled posts so you don't have to try and remember to post regularly (this is a great tool, particularly if you have a gig or album coming up).

- Change the 'call to action' button on your Facebook page to whatever you want people to do next – that may be book a ticket, buy an album or send an enquiry.

- Encourage people to like and share all the time. The more comments you achieve on your posts, the more views you will get organically. Bear in mind though that Facebook will probably try to limit your organic exposure to encourage you to advertise through them, so without boosted posts you may only get onto the timelines of around 2% of your followers.

- If you feel like your Facebook page isn't getting the traction you need, then you can pay to boost posts using Facebook Ad Manager. This is very effective if you are savvy about the demographics and locations you want to appeal to, and you can find lots of instructional videos to help you along the way.

- Consider whether you want to link all of your social media accounts or not.

- 'Facebook Live' is a great tool. You could take your audience on a backstage tour, or do an interview, or announce the results of a competition. All of this is very engaging content and will help build your followers. Keep videos nice and short (and don't forget to press 'save' when you're done, or it'll be gone forever!).

In general, it is getting harder and harder for organisations, bands and groups to gain organic exposure on social media. People complain about this, but it's not massively shocking that you should need to pay to market something you stand to make money out of.

Facebook is free to all users for personal use, and it will likely stay that way. But of course they will charge if you want to advertise your products and services through it, so as a result they will make it difficult for your brand to stand out organically.

It may cost a few quid to boost a post on Facebook, but if you compare that to the cost of any other advertising it is pretty minimal. Just make sure you get bang for your buck by swotting up on how best to boost **sponsored posts** first. You'll also learn by trial and error, so if you don't get the results you want first time then keep trying.

YouTube

You'll need to set up a YouTube channel as this is where you will save any good quality videos of you playing live, along with studio videos and/or lyric videos. Make sure this is linked up to your other social media channels and also linked to your website.

YouTube offer a course on how to set up a music channel. It's well worth doing this, as it can feel a little overwhelming to start with. And that way, you'll know that you're using 'best practice' to set the channel up. You'll learn a lot about attracting viewers and optimising your content along the way, too.

How often, when and what content to post

People often worry about 'overdoing it' on social media, and they have a point, to a certain extent. As much as you need to reinforce your message several times for it to be heard, space it out so you aren't bombarding people. Posting once a day is enough.

Consider some 'back-scratching'. It gets tedious if people are constantly self-promoting, and it can lead to people hitting the 'unfollow' button.

Share other bands' updates to show that you are supporting others' efforts, share interesting/funny content that's relevant in some way… basically give other people exposure through your channels. It will reap rewards as people will feel much more generous when it comes to sharing your posts back.

The single biggest mistake people (brands, bands and individuals alike) make on social media is to make it ALL ABOUT THEM. **Constant self-promotion will alienate people**.

The things that go wrong in life are often far more relatable or funny than the perfect bits. So if you have a tour mishap or an instrument falls to bits then share it – people like seeing the bad times almost more than they like seeing the good times (I don't know what that says about human nature!).

As a general rule keep **80% for conversational, funny and interesting posts, and about 20% for self-promotion**. Of course, conversational posts can still be promotion, for example some documentary-style posting about the making of your new album.

It's just that framed in this way it does not come across as constant and direct self-promotion, and therefore it's less pushy.

Followers like the more random side of a musician's life, so be on the lookout for photo opportunities whether you're recording, rehearsing or touring.

If you're in a geeky kind of mood, then dig around in your social media '**Insights**' page. Here you will find out more about your demographic, who is interacting with you and what else they might be into.

There's a wealth of intel here that may well help to inform your decisions when it comes to deciding who to target with sponsored advertising. It's quite interesting once you get into it.

Building followers

There are plenty of ways to increase your followers, and these are worth exploring because the first things a potential agent/manager/record label will look at is the number of followers you have on Facebook and the number of YouTube videos you have amassed.

These days, it honestly doesn't matter how many hundreds of people come to your gig if you have fewer than 1000 followers.

It's well worth spending some time on this. Ask your existing followers to like and share both your posts and your page – offer an incentive like a free CD or a pair of tickets to your next show (but make sure you follow through on the prize!).

Ask people to review you too. The more activity on your page, the more it will be visible to people.

Be inventive. The posts that get interaction on social media tend to be the curious, the strange, the funny, the original. Don't just say you're playing at some venue on Saturday and it'd be great to see everyone there – make it more engaging, more readable and more shareable too.

And always add an image or a video to a post – without one or the other the post just won't get noticed.

Other platforms

There are loads of online communities where you can upload your music and build your fan base, like **Bandcamp** and **Soundcloud**. When you are considering which platforms to use, consider the following questions which should help you make your mind up:

1. Which platforms are most popular amongst your peers and target audience?
2. What does the platform offer in terms of benefits for using?

You'll find that certain platforms are a natural fit for you, whereas others won't work for you. Focus on the one or two that you stand to generate the best results from, and build your fanbase.

If you want to learn more about how to leverage social media for musicians then there is a great resource here: https://sproutsocial.com/insights/social-media-for-musicians/

Social Media Campaigns

A strategic approach to social media can really help you maximise results, and also save you time as you can set it up to run automatically by scheduling posts. If you have got a big event coming up such as the release of new tour dates, then it's a great idea to build excitement by scheduling an announcement, and running a campaign throughout the tour.

Release a teaser a week or so before and get people wondering about what it is you're going to announce. Building suspense in this way works well and more and more bands are using it as a technique to maximise engagement when the announcement comes out.

Your teaser can be a video with some vague hints, or simply a post giving a time and date for people to be on the lookout for news and announcements.

In the meantime, you need to ensure that all of your resources are ready to go for when you go live. For a tour announcement that means tour posters, ticket links, live video clips... the works.

A strategic 'campaign' approach to social media is a good idea for lots of reasons. It keeps all of your messaging on-brand and consistent, and when it's set up to run itself you can have a few days away from social media knowing that everything is in hand and messages are still going out. Plan your content in advance so you know what is going out, and when.

Competitions

Social media competitions are a great way to boost engagement and build followers – and also to get more people to come to your gigs.

A simple *'like and share this post to be in with a chance of winning free tickets to our next gig'* will do the trick. Or you could get creative and make the competition a little more unique.

You could run a competition to get someone to design your next album cover, or a tour poster, or something for your next run of merch.

Whatever you do, make sure the winner is picked in a legitimate way – you can use online software to randomly generate a name or number. Then publicise the winner and congratulate them online so that the competition is seen as completely fair and transparent.

Membership Sites

I'm including this under 'social media', but really membership sites offer a whole lot more, to an audience that you know is already fully engaged with who you are and what you do. This is a very effective way of building and rewarding your online community's loyalty.

The recent pandemic has seen a huge surge in musicians using membership platforms such as Patreon to give their fans a different kind of experience for a monthly membership fee. This is a fantastic way of securing regular monthly income (the holy grail to the freelance musician), thereby enabling you to predict at least a slice of your income slightly more easily.

You give fans exclusive access to content, your community, and perhaps also insight into your creative process. You can put on exclusive online gigs for your most loyal fans, and perhaps even offer a live Q&A/backstage tour afterwards.

This is a great way of building meaningful connections with your fanbase and offering those who support you a little more for their money. There are usually various membership levels depending on the features you want to make use of.

CHAPTER FIVE: WEBSITE

This doesn't have to cost you much money. A lot of bands shy away from setting up a website because they don't have the necessary skills or budget, but this is changing fast.

Firstly, buy your domain name (this is easier than it sounds). Then choose a programme like Wix or SquareSpace – and there are plenty of others – to design your site. You can do this yourself and don't need to pay a web designer to do it for you. It can be daunting to get started but it's easy and intuitive once you get going.

You pay a bit of money for a theme/template and then the rest is up to you to populate/fill in the blanks. Having a decent logo, plenty of pre-written content and images etc to work with can help to speed up the process.

The Webpages

Keep the structure really simple – six main pages are enough. And keep the names of each page as short as possible (one word is great) as this will help with design and navigation around your website. Something like:

HOME / ABOUT / LIVE / PRESS / SHOP / CONTACT

Here's a little bit about each:

Home

Keep it simple – a few images, some words and your logo is fine.

People used to say that each page should have 300-ish words on it for Search Engine Optimisation (also known as SEO – more on that in a bit). But that's not the case anymore so don't write loads of words for the sake of it. Focus on a few short, snappy lines and good quality images.

You can add your Twitter feed to your home page to keep it looking fresh and up to date, and don't forget to add links to all your social media platforms somewhere obvious. Make it as easy as possible for people to stay in touch.

You could also add a newsletter sign-up form that pops up when people arrive on the home page. This can be done by linking with software such as Mailchimp which is a free and easy way of building a mailing list and sending regular newsletters to your fans.

Newsletters should be sent sparingly – focus on quality over regularity. Only send one when you have plenty of things to say, a new tour to promote, or a new album to launch.

(As a side note, if you are planning to send e-newsletters then it's a good idea to learn/brush up on the recent GDPR rules which have come into place (https://mailchimp.com/help/about-the-general-data-protection-regulation/). They shouldn't affect you too much, but it's worth having a working knowledge all the same.)

And finally, you'll be missing a trick if you don't feature your music prominently on your home page. Think of this page as your shop window – make sure your latest video is there to watch and any upcoming gigs are plugged.

About

This is where your killer 100-word bio goes.

Under that, write a little about each member of the band, because people will be interested in who you are, who else you've played, recorded and toured with and any other random facts about you all. Add pictures wherever possible, and keep every paragraph short and sweet. Don't use long sentences or too many clichés.

Live

This is where you list all of your upcoming gigs. Use a sensible, easy-to-navigate template for this. You don't need loads of info here, just the basics – venue, location, booking number and a link to tickets, and/or a Facebook event page.

Press

This is where you save anything and everything that someone will need if they are going to feature you in an article, promote your gig, or get involved in pretty much any other sort of way. It should include your band biography (a short version and a longer version), press photos, videos, poster templates, a high-res logo to download (black and white, and colour too) and anything else you have that will help to sell you.

Imagine you are promoting a gig – what would you need from the band? Make life easy for people who are booking you – they'll appreciate it and they'll probably book you again too.

Another thing that is useful to include in your press kit is an EPS version of your logo. An EPS file is a vector file of a logo. This is a logo that has no background, therefore being better for creating posters etc. If you can't create this yourself then it's a quick job for a designer to do it for you.

Here's the ultimate list of what should be included in your electronic press kit (sometimes known as EPK):

- High-res logo
- Up-to-date biography (short version and extended)
- Tour dates
- Links to music/downloads
- Photos and videos
- Press coverage
- Contact information

Note if you have a booking agent then they will usually carry all of this information on their website as opposed to yours. If this is the case, then a link to their website will suffice.

Shop

Here is where you sell T-shirts, CDs, downloads, merchandise… the works. Merch is a great way to boost income and it's worth getting as creative as possible when it comes to products. You can get items branded very easily from plenty of online suppliers (such as this one which I've used before with no issues: https://www.4imprint.co.uk/), and I've seen bands sell branded bottle openers, lighters, badges, even jockstraps!

The more products you can load onto this the better but make sure you use a decent e-commerce plug-in for this to ensure that the buying experience is as easy as possible.

The band Ferocious Dog has one of the most inventive merch stands both online and at gigs that I've seen. Check out their range of merchandise for plenty of great ideas (https://ferociousdog.co.uk/merch/).

If you don't have anything to sell yet, don't worry. Just ensure that the platform/template that you are using will allow you add a 'shop' facility whenever you are ready.

When building your stock, make sure that everything is top quality. It might be tempting to source a load of cheap tat and brand it up for mega profit margins, but complaints will come through thick and fast – and usually that will happen on social media for all to see. Invest in good quality, 100% cotton T-shirts and get them printed by someone who knows what they are doing. You want those T-shirts to last a long, long time – it's great advertising for your brand after all.

There will inevitably be some returns and complaints, so when this happens make sure it is dealt with swiftly and fairly.

Get some stickers made up with your band logo on them. It's a very cheap way of plastering your brand here, there and everywhere. Removable car stickers are great too.

Contact

Set up a dedicated band email address – a Gmail one or similar will look unprofessional. When you buy your domain name you will get associated email addresses to use. Add a mobile number for yourself or your booking agent. Make it easy for people to contact you. This is another place to remind people about your social media links too.

The more work you put into your website, the more it will work for you. So spend time writing great words, sourcing great photos and making sure it is up to date with all your latest gigs. If you're a bit of a writer then blog about your gigs, or life on the road, or your plans for your next album – anything.

The more content you load onto your site, the better. This will help with SEO – but do remember to proofread everything that gets added.

Search Engine Optimisation

And talking of SEO… this is what helps people find you through search engines such as Google. If getting to the first page of search engines for things like 'wedding bands in London' matters to you because people search on those sorts of terms to find you, then you need to get up to speed on SEO.

There used to be a load of tricks (called black-hat and grey-hat SEO) to beat the system, but these days the algorithms (the programs that run behind the search engines to make them work) are pretty smart, and they're constantly being updated too.

You don't need to worry about keywords these days; simply focus on good quality content that's well-written and typo-free. Then spend some time on your website's meta descriptions.

Meta What Now?

A meta description is a short sentence or two that appears under your domain name in search engine listings. It's a very short summary and if it's written well it can really help draw people towards your website.

Meta descriptions aren't as complicated as they sound and are easy enough to tweak yourself, so it's worth getting a working knowledge of SEO so you can optimise your site.

The key to SEO success is understanding what keywords people might use to find you. So if you're a party and wedding band based in Brighton, or a jazz band based in Edinburgh, then this sort of information needs to be in your meta descriptions.

Again, blogging will organically boost your SEO because search engines reward good, authoritative content. Don't worry about stuffing your content with keywords that people might use to find you – that doesn't work anymore and it might even work against you.

The Grammar Hammer

Weed any typos out of your website, and if this isn't your strong point then ask someone to do you a favour and proofread your site. Search engines love good grammar, and they hate typos. Poorly written content can make you look quite unprofessional too, so do spend time getting this right. Apps like Grammarly are great for spotting the obvious clangers.

Call to action

Every page should feature a clear 'call to action'. This is generally a clickable button that clearly and concisely tells people what to do next, and signposts them to the right place. For example, 'Join our mailing list', 'Book Tickets', 'Contact Us', or 'Shop Now'.

Aim to have a call to action (CTA) at the bottom of every page which will help your visitors navigate their way around your site. This is also good advice for your social media posts by the way.

CHAPTER SIX: PHOTOS AND VIDEOS

As part of your press kit you'll need great photos and videos (live and studio). In this section I'll cover off a little about both of these.

Photography

Firstly, you need a band photo. This is something you will see everywhere you go; it'll be on posters, you'll see it online and on venue websites. So it must be a) good quality, b) an accurate representation of who you are, and c) something that doesn't make you cringe when you see it repeatedly.

Work with an established photographer - sometimes you can find photographers who will help you for free in return for them being able to use your photos in their portfolio, or linking/crediting them on social media. Set up a photo shoot in an interesting place, and if you know anyone full of ideas then invite them along as 'Creative Director'.

Props, costumes and instruments can be used in the shoot if that works for you, or perhaps it might just be the group of you standing around looking cool/wistful/whatever look you're going for.

Be original. A photo of you all walking away or towards the camera carrying your instrument cases has been done a million times.

Once you've got your band photo sorted, some live images will also be useful. Often at gigs people will come along and take photos. Connect with them afterwards and ask them to tag you so you can see them.

Don't ever use these photos without their express permission; sometimes they will be happy for you to use them if you credit them, while other times they may want to charge for the use. Either way, make sure you're both happy with the deal before you use them for your own purposes.

Live photos are great because they are full of passion and capture a moment in time. If you know you have a big gig coming up where there will be a decent light show and a big audience, it's worth offering local photographers a pair of free tickets to come along and take some snaps.

Videos

Live videos of gigs are a great way of showing people what they can expect from your show. In this age of ubiquitous smartphones you won't be short of video footage, but this can be poor quality and shaky and just unprofessional.

Find a local videographer to come along to a big show and take some footage of you doing your thing. They might also at the same time carry out some interviews with you and perhaps take some documentary footage at the same time which can be edited down the line.

If you are releasing a single then a studio video can really help you promote it. Once your track is recorded, you can make the video as low-key or as big as you want with basic video editing software. Those who are savvy with technology can make videos themselves, and if that's not in your skill-set the chances are that you have friends who can help.

Add a twenty-second clip of your video on social media to pique interest, and then signpost people to your YouTube channel to watch the full video. This is important because you'll want to capture as many YouTube views as possible.

Videos are also a great way of documenting life on the road/backstage to share with your followers online. Keep videos very short – less than a minute ideally – in order to get as much engagement as possible. The funnier/sillier/more entertaining the better.

You could interview each other backstage or record a tour of the backstage facilities for example. Be as inventive as possible as videos are one of the most powerful ways to grab attention online. You can also make use of Facebook Live to stream gigs and snapshots of rehearsals etc too.

There are some exceptional examples of bands whose marketing depends almost entirely on their music videos. Check out this video by Ok Go (https://www.youtube.com/watch?v=dTAAsCNK7RA) which has been viewed over 46 million times - a great example of how a creative and original video can really give you the edge.

We may not all have their sort of budget, but it certainly gets you thinking...

CHAPTER SEVEN: MEDIA (DIGITAL, PRINT AND RADIO)

Your music needs to be heard by as many ears as possible, and the best way to make that happen is to push it on every channel you can think of. Away from your own website and social media etc, there are plenty of other places you can promote your band, and in this chapter, I'll cover off the main ones.

Digital

Digital or online media is probably the easiest and cheapest way to spread the word about your music. You really can take this as far as you want to go. When I say digital media I mean online magazines, review pages and online news sites. Remember, the people who run these platforms need content, so the easier you make it for them to promote you, the more you will pique their interest.

Attracting these platforms' interest will give you a lot of exposure and get your name in front of new audiences. Shoot for the ones that have the most followers and engagement to get the best results, and equally don't spend a lot of time trying to attract platforms with a low number of followers.

If you have a gig, an album or a tour to promote, then this is a great time to seek an editorial in an online music magazine. The best way to do this is to write a short, snappy cover email, then attach a good quality band promotional shot, a press release (around 2-300 words) and plenty of links to your social media and videos etc, along with a contact number for media enquiries and interviews etc.

If the press release is written well enough then you'll have done half their job for them – it is not uncommon for online platforms to publish your press release word-for-word, repackaged as an editorial. It saves them a lot of time, money and hassle to do it this way, so everybody wins. When writing your press release, write it in the <u>third person</u> and follow a format along these lines:

- Headline
- 150-word introduction, covering who, what, where, why and how.
- A short quote from you. For example, "Lead singer Alice Smith says, 'We can't wait to get out on the road and share our music with our fans. So much work has gone into this album and it's exciting to finally be able to share it'."
- Short summary at the end with links to whatever you want readers to do next, i.e. book tickets, buy the album, like the Facebook page etc, along with contact details.

Whenever you get any coverage at all in the online press, be sure to share the links across your social media platforms in order to boost hits to their webpage as much as possible. They will be keeping an eye on web hits, and if you generate a lot of visitors to their site then they will come back to you for more.

Another group of people to engage with online are the music bloggers. There are loads of people who enjoy blogging about music, and they are always looking out for content and new names to feature in their blogs. Build a relationship with a few that are relevant to you and you'll find that they can help you out a lot along the way.

Printed media

Printed media is local/national newspapers and magazines. It's really exciting to open up a newspaper or magazine and see your name in it, and it's a lovely thing to cut out and keep too. (Keep a box for this stuff – it's great to look back on).

As with online media, newspapers and magazines are always pleased to receive content that is usable without too much work. These people work on very tight deadlines and are always on the lookout for ways to fill column inches quickly.

Build a relationship with the music editor of your local newspaper and you'll find that they will give you plenty of opportunities to promote your gigs locally in their 'What's On' pages. Most of this content is then published online too.

Keep an eye out for any other local publications away from local magazines that might feature you too.

It's harder to get into the national music magazines, but it never hurts to try. Engage with them, share and comment on their content and put your name firmly on their radar.

Radio

Radio is still a great way to get yourself heard. And due to the sheer number of radio stations around it's easier than ever to make it happen.

BBC Introducing is a great way to start. It's easy to load your music onto their website, and they guarantee that everything will get listened to. If it grabs their interest you'll likely be invited onto a show to talk and/or play live, they will play your records and invite you play at some of their live events.

This is a relationship that needs careful nurturing; don't expect results overnight but instead play the long game, engage with them online and build a meaningful relationship with them.

There are plenty of other radio stations that you can target too, all of which are constantly looking for content to promote. As I keep coming back to, make it as easy as possible for these people to hear you, find out more about you and get in touch with you. Ensure you have a full press kit before you even think of approaching these people.

If you're going to do a radio interview then it's a great idea to watch some media training videos online. This is what the big stars do and it helps them get their message across without accidentally saying anything they didn't intend to.

Speaking eloquently on the radio is difficult; nerves can kick in and you can easily end up waffling, so remember to take deep breaths, listen more than you talk and don't force yourself into any corners.

In general, the more radio play you get the better. It's a very quick and easy way of reaching much bigger audiences, so spend time building relationships with DJs.

Royalties

There are entire books written purely on the subject of getting royalties paid for your work. The bottom line is that you can and should get paid every time your music is played, either on the radio or live. Signing up with PRS (https://www.prsformusic.com/) is relatively straightforward and you can register your music so that royalties get directed straight to you automatically.

PRS is a useful resource for all sorts of information so do sign up and familiarise yourself with how the systems works if you haven't already.

CHAPTER EIGHT: NETWORKING

Online networking is a wonderful way of connecting with people and getting word out about your music. I've covered a lot of this already as it's a vital tool for any band looking to increase their exposure.

But you must get out from behind your screen (if only for your own sanity!) and network in person with people. Getting to know fans in person is essential; they want to feel like they know you and that you recognise them when they come back to gigs time and time again. It's their reward for supporting you and it's essential that you say thank you.

When you're at a gig (whether it's your own or someone else's), spend time getting to know people. It's easy to appear an extrovert when you're on stage doing your thing, but many musicians are natural introverts in 'real-life', and they can find talking to people difficult. But hanging around at the end of gigs and getting to know people will pay dividends, and you'll meet some interesting characters along the way too.

If you're nervous about approaching someone then one way of combating that is to approach someone who is standing on their own. The chances are they are feeling as awkward as you are, and they'll appreciate you making the first move. From there, you can introduce that person to the next person that comes along, and so on. Before you know it, you'll know everyone in the room!

It's those seemingly innocuous conversations that can lead to all sorts of other things happening. Follow up any interesting conversations with an email afterwards so people know you've remembered them.

Get some business cards made up and carry them with you at all times. That way, whenever you get talking to people about your music you will be able to give them the details that they need to go away and look you up again at a later date.

The business card should be simple yet contain all the information people need: your band name, contact number, website and social media links. These can be done very cheaply and if you want to design it yourself then you can use a programme like Canva.

There are often music industry networking events held in most cities, so make it your business to go along and get to know people there. You'll meet agents, managers, other bands, promoters and record label representatives, and you'll learn a lot about the industry at the same time. Often the delegate list for these events is released in advance, so do your homework and research anyone you know you need to speak with.

This is when your 100-word 'elevator pitch' will come into its own. Rather than waffling on and then walking away wishing you'd said something completely different, have your answer rehearsed for when people ask you what you do.

There will be times when you come across someone that could be hugely influential to you. It goes without saying, but I'll say it anyway; don't blow your chances by being too pushy. Introduce yourself, ask them a question, listen to the answer but don't push your music on them, or make the conversation all about you. Instead, appeal to their ego and ask their advice on something, and see if there is a way you can give to them before receiving.

Jam sessions, singer/songwriter nights and showcase sessions are also a great way to meet not just fellow musicians but also a whole host of other interesting people too. Each of these has their own etiquette to follow, so if any of them are new to you then do some work finding out how they run first rather than risk an embarrassing if innocent faux pas.

Keep all the contact details that you collect when networking, no matter where you are or how irrelevant the connection may have felt at the time. And always follow up any referrals or useful conversations with a 'thank you' so they have your contact details too. You never know when you may need to look them up again.

Above all, when networking, remember to relax and be yourself. People are attracted to authentic, genuine people. There's nobody quite like you, so be proud of that and don't try to fit into any other moulds.

The single most effective thing you can do when networking whether online or in-person is to be a nice person. Do people favours; a bit of back-scratching goes a very long way and you'll be remembered as a nice/useful/kind/funny person to have around.

CHAPTER NINE: MAILING LISTS AND NEWSLETTERS

As I mentioned in the Website section, building a mailing list is a great way to build your marketing outreach. It means that when you have exciting news to announce, you have a ready-made list of email addresses to send it out to.

Always be on the lookout for ways to build your mailing list. Here are some ways you can do that:

- Add a pop-up to your website home page asking people to subscribe.
- Keep a mailing list on your merch desk at gigs to collect email addresses.
- Also at gigs, consider running a competition – people give you their email address to enter and at the end of the night a winner is drawn who gets a free T-shirt, album, etc.
- Add a call to action on your social media platforms directing people to sign up.
- Offer a free download of a song in return for signing up.
- Offer exclusive content and say they'll be the first to hear about new gig dates, releases etc if they sign up.
- Post regularly on social media asking people to sign up to stay in touch.

- Consider 'gated content' where you allow people access to a private streamed gig.

No matter how you collect email addresses, make sure it is completely clear what you will do with them. To stay on the right side of the new General Data Protection Regulations, make sure people who sign-up know they are opting in to receive regular newsletters, and that you won't share their data with anybody else.

GDPR is nothing to be scared of, and you won't be doing anything wrong as long as people are opting in and you're not acquiring their email address through any other means, or selling their data on either.

Programs like Mailchimp make all of this pretty easy, and you can create a branded opt-in form that you can use for your website. There are plenty of other platforms too; this is just the one I know and can therefore recommend.

For a crash course in building a mailing list, there are plenty of resources on their website – check this one out: https://mailchimp.com/resources/how-to-build-your-email-list/

When building your opt-in form, keep it really simple. You literally only need to know people's first name and email address, so don't scare anyone off by asking for addresses, dates of birth etc.

Regularity and Content of your eNewsletter

You shouldn't be sending out newsletters more regularly than once a month, and even this could be considered to be overkill. Instead, focus on fewer newsletters with better quality content. Any eNewsletter software will help you build your email based on many different templates available. You will be able to load your logo in and customise it to your brand colours.

After a short intro with a general update about what you've been up to and what's cooking, things you can include should fall into sections such as:

- Gig dates
- Album news
- Merchandise available
- Competition (a great opportunity to get people liking and sharing)
- Photos (new members, live gigs, new instruments).
- A big thank you to everyone who comes to gigs, and spreads the word.
- Share some news about other bands and their gigs too if you can – don't make it all about you. A little back-scratching goes a long way, and they'll likely return the favour.

There are plenty of other things you can include in your mailing too, but keep it relatively brief and engaging, and if you do nothing else make sure you ask someone to proofread and sense-check it for you before you hit 'send'.

A mailing list is a powerful tool. As opposed to social media, you can guarantee that your content is at least going to get seen, if not read, because you know it lands in people's inbox. Spend some time thinking of a snappy email subject line as this will boost the number of times the email gets opened.

You can then look at the insights to find out how many people have unsubscribed, how many bounces you've had, and weed out/change any incorrect email addresses. You can also get even more detailed information such as how many people have clicked on links in the eNewsletter.

It's a bit of a minefield but it's fascinating to start understanding how your audience behaves, what they like and what they don't.

Mailing lists and eNewsletters are a huge learning curve and it will take time to figure out what works for you best, but the sooner you start the better!

CHAPTER TEN: GETTING GIGS

Getting gigs is what it's all about. Prepping all of your marketing, photos, bios and videos, and recording your music is all for this moment – playing live.

Getting started

It's easier than you'd think to get started. People who run jam nights and showcase sessions are always looking for something new and interesting. You may end up playing for free a little bit, but if this works in your favour then go for it. Be wary of anyone who asks you to play for free if they are making a lot of money out of the event though. I've covered fees earlier in this book so no need for any more on that now.

Depending on the type of music you play, you may find that weddings and parties are a good place to get paid gigs. Party bands work very well in the evenings, but if your music is more chilled then it may be suitable as background music for daytime events. String quartets, jazz bands and folk instrumental outfits work well for occasions such as this.

Every town and city has music venues, some of which may play host to some big names but there are always opportunities to get involved with these as a support band. Keep an eye on regular events at these venues – most run a 'local band night' or even a 'Battle of the Bands'. Watch local press to see where other bands like yours are playing – and network and connect with bands in a similar genre to you to see if there might be opportunities to pass gigs each other's way.

Folk sessions

Sessions are brilliant training grounds for folk musicians as well as ideal places to find people to jam with. You may feel out of your comfort zone at first, but you'll reap the benefits. Don't let one bad experience put you off—try out loads of sessions and you'll see how different they can be.

However, sessions can be daunting if you haven't been to one before, so here are some general folk session 'dos and don'ts':

Do...

- Turn up on your own—it's fine and lots of other people will too.
- Introduce yourself.
- Play from written music if it makes you feel more confident, but aim to play by ear.
- Ask the name of a tune once it has finished and write it down to learn if you like it.
- Start the odd tune/set off if you feel confident enough, but choose one you think people may know to begin.
- Learn to recognise basic guitar chord shapes—it is useful for following guitarists' chords when you don't know a tune.
- Improvise - if you don't know the tune, try a basic rhythm on an open string that fits.
- Always have your fiddle handy at festivals in case you stumble across a good session.
- Ask about anything else going on in the area.

Don't...

- Be nervous.
- Forget to tune-up first.

- Get your instrument out unless you intend to play – you may get put on the spot.
- Expect to be able to join in with every tune.
- Talk through a tune or a song you don't know. Listen instead.
- Dominate.
- Play too fast.
- Drink too much and compromise your playing.
- Handle others' instruments without asking first.
- Forget to leave your instrument in a safe place if you go to the bar.

Busking

Busking is one of the best ways to start playing live. It'll sharpen up your skills and help you learn how to attract and hold the attention of an audience who, let's face it, aren't there to see you!

By far the hardest part of busking is playing the first note. I find this horribly daunting and I'm just waiting for someone to walk by and tell me to shut up! But the reality is that, unless you're terrible, your music will brighten any street, and any shopper's day.

Pick a busy place (pedestrianised places work really well) and get set up. There are a few minor bits of busking etiquette that I'll mention here in case useful.

- Make sure you don't need a busking permit before you start playing. Some city centres insist on one, and you can easily check this online.
- Don't play for more than an hour or so; after that move on.
- Be courteous to and support other buskers, and street sellers such as Big Issue sellers. Often you can strike a deal where one of you uses the 'patch' while the other goes off and gets lunch for example.

- If you're playing outside a shop, stick your head in first and ask them if they mind. They usually won't, in fact you'll probably brighten their day and attract customers too. Just don't stand too close to the door.
- Smile and enjoy yourself. You'll likely get anything from lighthearted banter through to full-on abuse levelled at you. You'll get a few nutters and you may get told to move on. It's not easy but it's character-building, and it'll build your resilience for performing live.

Pub gigs

Pub gigs can be a great way of earning some cash too and picking up a few new fans – again, if your music suits that sort of environment. Playing in pubs can be a lot of fun; it's an intimate setting where you are generally very close to your audience.

But pubs can also be awful places to play. If your music isn't right for the venue then people will vote with their feet; punters generally don't have to pay to get into a pub gig so if your music isn't doing it for them they will simply move on to the next place.

And conversely, if your music is going down *too* well then you may well find that your space in the room is invaded by over-eager and slightly drunk dancers.

This can be a challenge, especially with all that expensive gear around you. Always use monitors as they are a great natural 'barrier' between you and the audience, and make it clear where your stage boundaries are to try and keep the dancers at a healthy distance.

Only agree to gigs in a pub if you are sure that it's the right place for you to play, otherwise nobody will end up having a good time, the tills won't fill (and filling tills is the main reason why you have been booked to play) and it will reflect badly on your reputation.

Festivals

Festivals are another place to target. Be realistic about where your band will fit into the hierarchy bearing in mind your genre and current popularity. Be patient – bands who start at the bottom can work their way up the line-up if they are patient enough.

Festivals tend to book bands every other year to keep the line-up fresh, otherwise they look like they are recycling a format. So if you go down well one year at a festival, don't then be despondent if they don't then book you the following year.

Instead, make a note to stay in touch with the bookers, and check in with them at the time they will be considering their line-up for the next year (generally festivals book at least six months ahead of the date itself).

House gigs

There is a growing trend in certain areas of music for house gigs. These are put on by people who love your music in their own house. They sell tickets to their friends and put on a night where they can all socialise together and enjoy some music, generally in a 'sit down and listen' scenario.

It's a beautifully intimate way of presenting your music, and what you may lack in terms of light shows or massive audiences you will make up for by creating a memorable evening that's full of magic moments.

There are various groups on Facebook where you can network with other musicians who run house gigs, and also the people who like to host them. You can plot a tour on house gigs alone, you can expect to earn enough money from ticket sales to make it worth your while, and the gig will include food and refreshments for you at the very least – if not accommodation for the night.

House gigs are a great way of building your network as there are loads of opportunities to get to know people on a one-on-one basis. Once you're on the 'inside' and if your music suits the occasion you'll find there are plenty of lovely evenings to be had.

Support gigs

Another good way of getting out there is to connect with a band who are the next level up to you, and offer to support them. Keep an eye out for bands who regularly tour and who you would realistically suit as their support band. You can expect to get paid something for support tours, but not a huge amount.

The benefits of this include playing to a much larger audience than you may be used to, and getting to know bigger venues who may later book you in your own right.

Word-of-Mouth Referrals

If people like your music then ask them to tell their friends! Word-of-mouth referrals are one of the best ways to get you heard by more and more people.

The folk/roots band Show of Hands took a uniquely creative approach to this word-of-mouth idea. A while ago in an age when everyone was trying to protect their music from being accessed for free, refusing to add it to Spotify and frowning on people making copies of CDs, these guys did the opposite. They sold CDs at gigs and actively encouraged people who bought them to make copies for their friends.

It was a generous offer and people liked their refreshing approach. The way the band saw it, their friends may get a free album but once 'recruited' these people would come to shows time and time again, and buy albums, and tell *their* friends.

It worked, because Show of Hands are one of the biggest acoustic bands around, and have filled the Royal Albert Hall several times over.

Moving up the ranks

The better you get and the more people that start coming to your gigs, the better those gigs that come your way will be. At this point it's a good idea to start thinking about agents and managers.

The good ones will be attracted by bands who have a respectable number of social media followers and YouTube hits, and they'll also be tempted by any band who can prove that they can sell plenty of tickets to live shows.

There will be plenty of people who 'say' they can manage you or help get you gigs, but vet them carefully. A lot of people say they can when they can't; they don't know the industry well enough and/or they don't have the connections.

The better your marketing, the more impressive you will look to people who can help you. They will be looking at things like your website, your social media and your videos.

They will also be looking carefully at ticket sales and listening carefully to what people say about you too, so that's when those referrals will really come through for you.

By now I'll be starting to sound like a stuck record, but if you want to attract the highest quality managers and agents, make it easy for them! You are their product, so turn out the very best music you can, get your marketing tied up, build your audience and they'll find it impossible to resist you.

I asked a few booking agents and managers what they looked for when considering signing a new act to their roster. Interestingly (and perhaps reassuringly too), while online statistics and ticket sales help a lot, they each said that it mainly came down to gut instinct.

Vicky Whitlock from **Firebrand Music** said:

"It's a little more about gut instinct than figures. But I have to like the band. I can't sell something I wouldn't listen to, but then I'm not a salesman so that might be personal. Good Facebook/Twitter activity and engagement is critical, and a good website. Preferably the band should be their primary focus.

They need to have done their own booking for some time - I need them to have walked the walk so they understand and appreciate what I do.

They need a 'driver' - someone who is business-focused and gets the need for strategy and promotion."

Steve Knightley of **Show of Hands** has worked in the industry for decades and there is little he doesn't know about the art and science of putting on a show. He says,

"I reckon to attract representation the act has put in so much groundwork they are almost self-sufficient. Then, when they possess that mindset, they are able to see the value of that extra 25% you can provide to take them to the next level. It's also useful if an act thinks they have something 'meaningful' and 'important' to say."

From garage band to professional outfit

If things go well and your band proves popular, then getting gigs will start to get a lot easier, and people will start coming to you rather than the other way around. The challenges at this point change somewhat. From now on, it's all about getting the *right* gigs and not getting sent off on a tangent.

At this point you'll probably have attracted the help of a manager who will help you take a more strategic approach to getting gigs. They and you will be looking for gigs that offer the most exposure at venues and festivals which carry weight in the industry. You will likely butt heads with your manager from time-to-time, as conflicting priorities can sometimes be at play.

For example, imagine you are offered a three-month stint in a holiday destination to entertain tourists. You may be swayed by the money and the guaranteed work, whereas your manager may feel that this strays too far off your strategic mission, and is a waste of time.

The secret to a good relationship with your manager, as is the case with every relationship, is communication. Keep an open and honest dialogue running and don't be afraid to speak your mind.

Rather than gigging relentlessly, a strategic approach helps you step-change from a local band that's ubiquitous and possibly underappreciated to a nationally/internationally touring band that is constantly reaching new audiences.

Your manager/agent will have built relationships with venues and festivals around the UK and beyond and they will begin to build tours that take you out of your usual haunts. These tours are focused and strategic, and they should pay well too. At this stage, gig contracts that you sign will prevent you from playing within a 20ish mile radius of their venue. Be wary of this so you don't end up stepping on anyone's toes.

A touring schedule helps you regain control of your diary. If you can plot two or three reasonably sized tours a year, this then frees you up to write, record, rehearse and create in the space in between. It's easy to think you can do all these things while you are touring, but the reality is that there is little downtime between gigs, sound checks and travel.

These gaps in your diary are also really useful for providing some much-needed headspace. You can step away from things for a while and think objectively about the direction in which you're going, and a little space from the things you love now and again is a healthy thing.

Of course, if you are planning these tours then you'll need to ramp your marketing up even further, and also make your promotion incredibly strategic. But the good news is that by then there should be a little wriggle-room in the budget to buy in the necessary help.

CHAPTER ELEVEN: POST-COVID AND BEYOND

Of course, the world has changed significantly throughout 2020. While the creative industries have suffered in so many ways, and careers have been unfairly decimated, I believe there is still room for optimism.

The music industry **is** a viable industry, and it always will be.

2020 has been a stark reminder to us all of both the importance and magic of music – particularly live music. There is an enormous appetite and a renewed appreciation for it.

Audiences and musicians alike will never take another note for granted. We all need the human connection that only music can deliver.

While restrictions are still in place, it's time to get organised. Set out your stall online, write more music, build your presskit and do as much as you can to sharpen up your marketing, so that when venues open up and restrictions are lifted you can hit the ground running.

The live stream market may be flooded, but it's a great way of remaining visible and connected to your audience.

It may not feel like it, but live music will return bigger, better and stronger than ever. We have to believe this. The need for music is innate in us all and it will have a huge part to play in healing the cracks in society as things return to whatever the new normal may be.

At the time of writing, none of us really know what that will look like yet, but I hold on to the hope that we will play and sing and dance together, totally carefree again soon.

Get out there and show the world what you can do, and don't stop until it listens!

RESOURCES

Here are some resources that you may find useful when it comes to marketing your music. All links were correct at the time of going to print.

- Arts Council England - https://www.artscouncil.org.uk
- BBC Introducing - https://www.bbc.co.uk/introducing
- PRS for Music - https://www.prsformusic.com/
- PPL - https://www.ppluk.com/
- ISM - https://www.ism.org/
- The Musicians' Union - https://musiciansunion.org.uk/
- GDPR Guidelines - https://www.gov.uk/government/publications/guide-to-the-general-data-protection-regulation
- I haven't mentioned individual platforms as there are so many, but there's a pretty comprehensive list here: https://takelessons.com/blog/music-resources-z15

ABOUT THE AUTHOR

Olivia Dunn

Olivia Dunn is a fiddle player by night and Head of Marketing and Communications for a management consultancy by day.

She has spent years playing, touring and recording with bands such as Mad Dog Mcrea and the Phil Beer Band. She's done her time in the back of Transit vans and sleeping on sofas while pursuing her musical dreams.

She's also worked as a booking agent and promoter and has generally taken responsibility for the marketing of any band she's played in.

These days Olivia still plays regularly around her family commitments.

As Head of Marketing and Communications for Halpin, a management consultancy for the higher education sector, Olivia applies her marketing knowledge to manage the firm's brand identity, consistency and messaging, and manages all internal and external communications.

Olivia lives in Devon with her partner, their daughter Lily, and numerous cats, guinea pigs and goats.

Printed in Great Britain
by Amazon